T0417820

THE INUIT

PEOPLE, CULTURE, AND HISTORY

by Tia Tidwell

CAPSTONE PRESS

a capstone imprint

Author Dedication
For my aana and taata Lela Kivaalook and Noah Katairoak Ahgook

Published by Capstone Press, an imprint of Capstone
1710 Roe Crest Drive, North Mankato, Minnesota 56003
capstonepub.com

Library of Congress Cataloging-in-Publication Data is available on the Library of Congress website.

ISBN: 9798875208348 (hardcover)
ISBN: 9798875208294 (paperback)
ISBN: 9798875208300 (ebook PDF)

Summary: Inuit traditions, culture, and history are showcased through engaging text, sidebars, activities, maps, and more.

Editorial Credits
Editor: Erika L. Shores; Designer: Heidi Thompson; Media Researcher: Rebekah Hubstenberger; Production Specialist: Tori Abraham

Image Credits
Alamy: Danita Delimont, 27, North Wind Picture Archives, 10, Paul Couvrette, 28, ton koene, 17, Tribune Content Agency LLC, 23; Associated Press: Rashah McChesney, 16; Getty Images: Andrew Burton, 20, 22, Bettmann, 25 (bottom), Erik Hill/Anchorage Daily News/Tribune News Service, 8, iStock/choicegraphx, 26, Laura Patterson/CQ Roll Call Archive, 15, Layne Kennedy, 5, OLIVIER MORIN/AFP, 25 (top), ZU_09, 9; Jonathan Butzke/Talking Circle Media, 12; Kendra Mack for Ilisaġvik College, 7; Library of Congress: Prints and Photographs Division/Carpenter Collection, 13; Newscom: Peter Langer/ DanitaDelimont.com/"Danita Delimont Photography," 18; Photo Courtesy Tia Tidwell, cover; Shutterstock: BlueBarronPhoto, 19, heenal shah, 4, IhorM, 29, MaraZe, 21 (textured paper), Runrun2 (brush stroke), front and back cover, spine, 1

Printed and bound in the USA. 006307

TABLE OF CONTENTS

Words in **bold** are in the glossary.

ABOUT THE INUIT

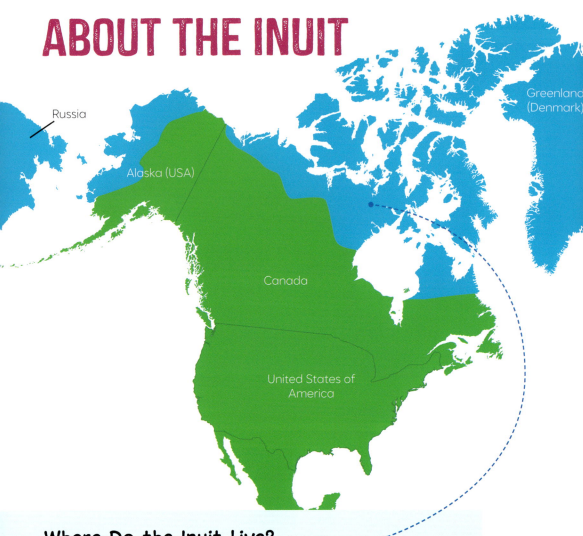

Russia

Greenland (Denmark)

Alaska (USA)

Canada

United States of America

Where Do the Inuit Live?

Inuit means "people" and "nunaat" is their homeland. Inuit live on the land around the Arctic Ocean. The Inuit have lived in the Arctic for thousands of years. Their homelands are now called the United States, Canada, Greenland, and Russia.

Inuit Are Indigenous Peoples
What does it mean to be Indigenous?

Indigenous people have lived sustainably connected to a land base for time immemorial, or as long as time has been remembered. That means Indigenous people and their **culture** are interconnected to their homelands. Sustainably connected means Indigenous people lived in balance with the land around them. Often Indigenous people would move to different places throughout the year and did not take too much from any single **environment** to survive.

Inuit Communities

Inuit share similar culture and languages around the **circumpolar** Arctic. But the Inuit nation is made up of diverse communities, people, and language dialects. A dialect means that the language varies depending on geographic region. In Alaska, the two largest Inuit cultural groups are Iñupiat and Yup'ik. About 180,000 Inuit live in Alaska, Canada, Greenland, and Russia.

AN INUIT CELEBRATION

The beat of drumsticks on round oil-cloth and animal-skin drums fill the air. Along with the drumming is the sound of Iñupiat songs. It is time for the Inuit celebration called Kivgiq (kiv-ghik). Dance groups of children, adults, and Elders perform for the gathered communities in front of them. The dancers' hand motions tell stories about Inuit life.

Kivgiq is an ancient tradition. Iñupiaq communities would send runners to invite neighboring communities to gather and celebrate harvests. Kivgiq is a celebration with singing, drumming, dancing, and gift giving. Kivgiq is a time when Inuit people gather to share and strengthen their relationships with each other. They honor their cultural identity.

Kivgiq took place for hundreds of years before being stopped by Christian missionaries in the early 1900s. Missionaries and government officials attempted to put an end to all traditional ceremonies. In 1988, Utqiaġvik's mayor George Ahmaogak worked to bring back Kivgiq for the first time in 70 years. Inuit Elders were interviewed to learn how Kivgiq should be done. Today, Kivgiq is held every two years.

Dancing is an important part of Kivgiq.

INUIT HISTORY

Inuit people in Alaska and Canada have always been connected to the rest of the world through trade and kinship. In 2004, blue trade beads from Venice, Italy, were found in the Brooks Range of Alaska at Punyik Point. The beads had arrived there in the mid-1400s.

Significant contact between Europeans and Alaskan Natives began in 1741. A Russian **expedition** was led by Vitus Bering. During this time, nations such as Russia used the international law of the Doctrine of Discovery to claim lands belonging to Indigenous peoples. The Doctrine of Discovery stated that land not lived on by Christians could be claimed by people ruled by Christian kings or queens.

Villagers from Quinhagak, Alaska, look at an amber trade bead found near their village.

The Doctrine of Discovery became law in the Americas through a U.S. Supreme Court case in 1823. The court's decision was used to justify the claiming of Indigenous land by European nations in the Americas.

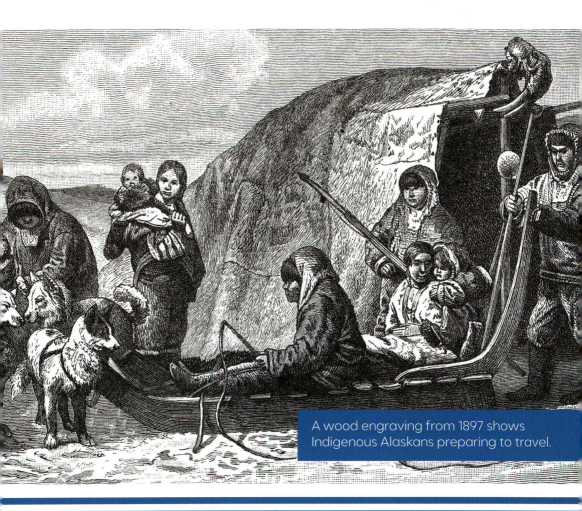

A wood engraving from 1897 shows Indigenous Alaskans preparing to travel.

St. Michael Redoubt was a trading post built in 1833 by the Russian-American Company in Alaska.

Early **colonizers** claimed Indigenous peoples' land under the Doctrine of Discovery by mapping, leaving things like flags or possession plates behind, or by building forts. In Alaska, early Russians left iron plates engraved with the message "country in possession of Russia" along Alaska's coastlines. This was done to show other nations, not Indigenous people, that Russia had been there first.

In 1867, Russia sold Alaska to the United States. They used the Doctrine of Discovery to claim they had the right to sell Alaska. The Russians never told the Indigenous people in Alaska that they had claimed their land as their own. Inuit homelands in Canada were claimed by Great Britain through the same Doctrine of Discovery.

During early colonization, Inuit people suffered. Colonizers brought diseases Inuit never had before. These diseases caused many deaths. Gifts from the land, like salmon and whales, had kept them alive for thousands of years. But now they were taken and used by colonizers to make themselves richer.

In the 1800s and 1900s, hundreds of thousands of Indigenous children, including Inuit children in the United States and Canada, were removed to **residential** boarding schools. They were taken away from their families and homelands. The goal of the boarding schools was to separate Indigenous children from their culture and language. These would be replaced with English customs and language.

At boarding schools, children were punished for speaking their language and practicing their culture. Schools were run by the federal governments of the United States and Canada and Christian churches. During this time, Inuit cultural practices and ceremonies were against the law.

Alberta Schenck

Alberta Schenck was an Inuit teenager living in Nome, Alaska, where she fought against segregation and helped to pass the Alaska Equal Rights Act of 1945. Schenck worked at a movie theater where seating was segregated by race. She spoke out against it. She was fired. She returned to sit in the "whites only" section. She refused to move. Schenck was then arrested and spent the night in jail. Her story was told to Alaska's lawmakers and helped ensure the equal rights act passed.

A group of Alaskan Native children at the Sheldon Jackson School, a residential boarding school, in Sitka, Alaska

Inuit communities are still working to heal from the harm that began in these schools. Inuit Elder Jim LaBelle Sr. is a residential school survivor who works with the National Native American Boarding School Healing Coalition. Many others are working to restore Native languages and traditional practices.

In Alaska, removal to residential boarding schools ended when 27 teenagers sued the state in 1972. The teens won their case in 1976 and proved the state had failed to provide education in their communities.

Timeline

1493	The Catholic Church issues the Doctrine of Discovery.
Late 1500s	The English begin exploring the Arctic.
1700s	Commercial whalers enter the Arctic.
Late 1700s	Commercial fur hunters spread throughout the Arctic.
1867	Russia sells Alaska to the United States.
1878	First residential boarding school established in Sitka, Alaska.
1879	U.S. government allows force to remove children from their families to attend boarding schools.
1883-1978	The Religious Crimes Code bans Indigenous dancing, ceremonies, and traditional healing practices.
1900	An influenza and measles outbreak causes the death of at least one quarter to one half of Inuit in Alaska.
1939	Inuit begin to be relocated and placed in permanent settlements by the Canadian government.
1944	The Canadian government forces Inuit to carry identification tags with their identification number.
1951	First government regulated residential school for Inuit children in Nunavut/Northwest Territories opens.
1953-55	High Arctic Relocation Program is created by the Canadian government to move Inuit families to northern Nunavut.
1971	Inuit Tapiriit Kanatami is founded by seven Inuit communities to protect the rights and interests of Inuit in Canada.
1972	The U.S. recognizes the rights of Alaska Natives to hunt marine mammals in the Marine Mammal Protection Act.
1977	Inuit Circumpolar Council organizes to promote Inuit rights and interests internationally.
1999	Nunavut, meaning "Our Land" in Inuktitut, is established furthering independence for Inuit in Canada.
2009	Inuit leaders in Alaska, Canada, Russia, and Greenland work to create "A Circumpolar Inuit Declaration on Sovereignty in the Arctic."

Inuit have a long history of **resilience** and thriving in their Arctic homelands. In 1977, Eben Hopson of Utqiaġvik (Barrow, Alaska) founded the Inuit Circumpolar Council (ICC) to combine Inuit talents to protect the Inuit way of life. The goals of the ICC are to strengthen unity among the Inuit circumpolar region. It promotes Inuit rights and protects Arctic land and waters.

In 2009, Inuit leaders in Alaska, Canada, Russia, and Greenland worked together to create "A Circumpolar Inuit Declaration on Sovereignty in the Arctic." This is a statement from the Inuit whose home has always been in the circumpolar Arctic on Inuit Nunaat. The Inuit have been living in these lands and using the Arctic waters for as long as remembered, even before anyone started written history. Inuits' special knowledge and experience of the Arctic land and waters and their language help them live their unique way of life. Even though the Inuit live in many different places, they are united as a single people.

William L. Hensley

Iġġiaġruk William L. Hensley was an influential leader who fought for Indigenous land claims. He worked for the passage of the 1971 Alaska Native Claims Settlement Act. It was one of the largest and most important Indigenous land claims in U.S. history. He also helped found the Alaska Federation of Natives to provide a voice in politics for Indigenous people in Alaska.

INUIT CULTURE

Culture is made up of things people can see on the outside, like clothing and tools, as well as things on the inside people cannot see, like values and beliefs. Culture is a part of who someone is. Just like all cultures, Inuit culture has changed and continues to change over time.

Inuit culture is shaped by the Inuit peoples' values. For example, the inland Iñupiat people of the Brooks Range call their values Ilitqusiat. Ilitqusiat means "those things that make us who we are." Some of the values guiding the culture are respect and love for each other, Elders, and children. Sharing, cooperation, humility, and responsibility to the community are very important. There is a deep respect for nature and important hunting traditions. It is important for Iñupiat people to learn their language and know their family and kin. They believe everything is connected.

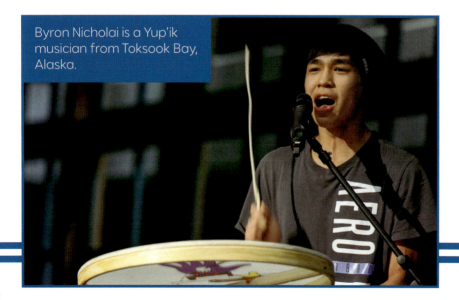

Byron Nicholai is a Yup'ik musician from Toksook Bay, Alaska.

Inuit Language

Inuit people share language. But it has many different dialects. Although Inuit people can usually communicate with one another across the circumpolar Arctic, many words are distinct to their geographic region.

Here are some words from the Nunamiut dialect of Iñupiaq language:

aana (ah-nah)—grandma

alaapa (ah-la-pah)—It is cold!

nunuk (nuh-nuk)—polar bear

quyanaqpak (kai-yan-ak-pak)—Thank you very much!

taata (dah-da)—grandpa

tuttu (too-too)—caribou

RESPECT FOR NATURE

Inuit people know the land is their older relative. The land cares for its people. Everything they are and have is a gift from the land. Inuit people know they have a responsibility to respect nature. Inuit are a part of nature and nature is their home. Nature is not some far-off place that a person goes to. Nature is everywhere a person is.

In the Arctic, many Inuit live in rural villages with small populations. Some of these communities are not connected by roads. One community is Anaktuvuk Pass. It is home to about 400 people. It can only be reached using small bush planes or snow machines. Many Inuit continue to live a subsistence lifestyle. They get their food and medicine directly from the land.

Children playing outdoors in Rankin Inlet, Nunavut Territory, Canada.

Anaktuvuk Pass is a village in the Brooks mountain range of Alaska.

Living a subsistence lifestyle means a lot of food and materials are hunted and gathered. For example, a caribou is hunted for its meat. Its hide can be used to make kamiks (boots). Caribou hair can be tufted into art and jewelry. Many kinds of wild plants and berries are harvested during summer and fall and stored to be eaten in winter.

Inuit eat a combination of food that is shipped north in small planes and food that comes from hunting and gathering. Successful hunters are responsible for sharing their catch and making sure everyone has enough. Food gathered and hunted from the land keeps Inuit healthy.

An Inuit Recipe

Inuit harvest fish like arctic char, whitefish, and salmon during the spring and summer and then preserve it by freezing, canning, or drying and smoking it.

FISH DIP

Ingredients

- 2 cups cooked or dried fish
- ¼ cup mayonnaise or preserved seal oil
- small onion, chopped
- ½ cup celery, chopped
- salt and pepper

Instructions

1. Combine the cooked or dried fish with the mayonnaise or preserved seal oil in a small bowl.

2. Add the chopped onion and the chopped celery.

3. Add salt and pepper to taste.

4. Eat and enjoy on top of crackers.

RESPECT FOR ELDERS AND LOVE FOR CHILDREN

Inuit people respect their Elders because they are the teachers and leaders. When gathering food from the land, some should always be shared with the Elders. The land watches Inuit people to make sure they are showing respect for its gifts by sharing.

Inuit children are named after respected Elders. The hope is children will pass on the Elders good traits, such as humility, knowledge of the land, and leadership skills.

Elders teach valuable lessons. Elder Sarah James teaches that when everyone older is treated as an Elder and everyone younger as a youth, then everyone in a community is honored and cared for.

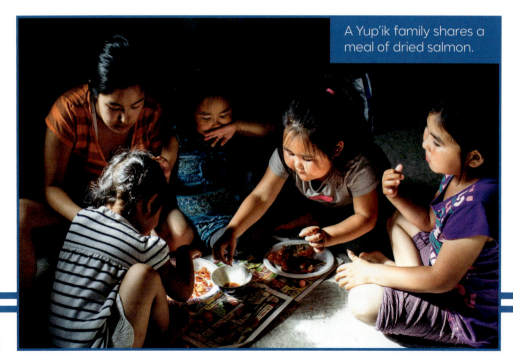

A Yup'ik family shares a meal of dried salmon.

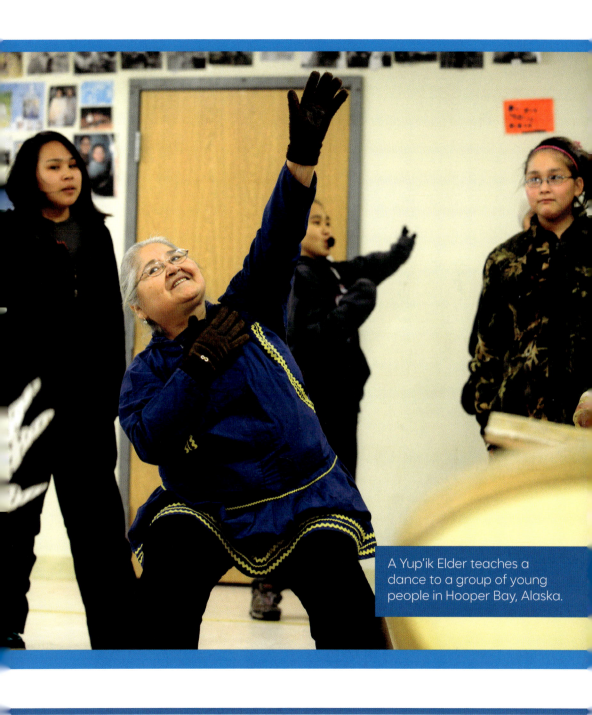

A Yup'ik Elder teaches a dance to a group of young people in Hooper Bay, Alaska.

HUNTING TRADITIONS

When an Inuit hunter catches their first animal, they gift the meat to an important Elder in their life. When an animal gives its life to an Inuit hunter, the Inuit respect the animal by using and sharing every part and speaking their thanks for the gift.

The animals hunted depend on the type of land. In mountain areas, such as Anaktuvuk Pass, Inuit rely on caribou, moose, mountain sheep, fish, ducks, and geese. In coastal areas, Inuit hunt whales, seals, and land animals, such as caribou and birds.

Hunters once used dogs and sleds. Now they use snow machines and argos. Traditionally, Inuit would move across the land to different places depending on the season. When whole communities moved, dogs were used to help carry belongings. Now that Inuit stay in one place all year, snow machines and argos are used to travel to camps for hunting and gathering.

Hunters used to use bows, arrows, and spears. Most hunters use guns now. However, the values of only taking what is needed, never wasting, and providing for the community are the same.

An Inuit hunter stands on the snowy tundra near an Arctic village in Greenland.

Uyaġak Howard Rock

Uyaġak Howard Rock was an Iñupiaq artist who started the newspaper, *Tundra Times*, in 1962. His goal was to keep Alaska Natives informed about issues that affected them. He helped get local and national support in the fight against the U.S. government's Project Chariot. The project pushed to create a deepwater port by using explosives near Cape Thompson, Alaska.

CLOTHING AND TOOLS

The Arctic can be very cold, so the Inuit made innovative clothing to keep warm. The amauti is a **parka** with a pouch in the back to carry a baby. There is a belt around the parka's waist for support.

Traditional clothing was made using animal skins. Today, many of the same designs are created using all kinds of fabric. Qaspeqs or atikłuks are summer parkas. Traditionally, some were made using seal guts to make them waterproof. Today, they are usually made of cotton. Many Inuit, Native, and nonnative people wear this fashionable and functional clothing in the Arctic.

Special tools and gear were also needed to survive in the Arctic. An ulu is a knife that can be used for everything from preparing food to sewing. People also used an ulu for trimming snow for an igloo (or snow house). Ulus used to be made with bone or ivory handles and slate blades. Modern ulus are usually still made with bone and ivory handles, but with steel blades.

Iggak, or sun goggles, are carved from ivory or bone to protect eyes from the sun reflecting on snow and ice. Modern-day sunglasses were inspired by Inuit iggak.

An Inuit woman in Nunavut, Canada, wears a ceremonial parka.

HONORING INUIT CULTURE

The Inuit have lived in the Arctic for thousands of years. They have a strong connection to their land and work to live in balance with their environment and communities. Inuit celebrate their traditions and culture with events like Kivgiq, where they dance, sing, and share food with their friends and family.

Inuit people faced many challenges in the past. They were forced to suppress their culture and language in residential boarding schools. But the people have worked hard to reawaken traditional cultural practices and languages. Today, they continue to honor their values and culture. They protect their land and make sure their stories and ways of life are remembered and shared.

Kenojuak Ashevak

Kenojuak Ashevak was a famous Inuit artist in Canada and a leader of modern Inuit art. She was born in 1927. Ashevak first learned traditional crafts from her grandmother. In her 20s, she began carving and drawing. Later, she became known for her graphic works. Much of her art is of owls and other birds. Ashevak's designs have been featured on postage stamps and Canadian money. She died in 2013.

An Origin Story

Every group of people have stories of how they came to be as a people. Inuit nation is made up of many smaller groups of people with distinct origin stories. This is one origin story that belongs to the Nunamiut people in Anaktuvuk Pass. It is based on a retelling by Nunamiut Elder and storyteller Elijah Kakinya.

A big flood came, and everything was covered by the ocean. The people were only able to hunt whales. When they were out in an umiak, they would see a little area with grass on it rising to the surface. They tried to catch it in their umiaks and kayaks. They tried to catch it with spears and snares but could not.

Then Raven set out in his kayak and speared it. As he speared it, it slowly came into view, with flowers on it. Raven gave a victory cheer, and the ocean began to recede, stranding the animals. The people riding in kayaks and umiaks found themselves on land. Worms and big snakes started wiggling from the land toward the ocean. The sea animals went back to the ocean swimming along the tracks of the snakes and worms. Thus, Raven secured the land for us.

Glossary

circumpolar (suhr-kuhm-POH-lur)—the areas around Earth's poles

colonizer (KAH-luh-nye-zur)—a nation or government that claims a territory other than its own

culture (KUHL-chur)—the traditions, beliefs, and behaviors that a group of people share

Indigenous (in-DIJ-eh-nus)—the first to live in a place

environment (in-VY-ruhn-muhnt)—the natural world of the land, water, and air

expedition (ek-spuh-DI-shuhn)—a journey with a goal, such as exploring or searching for something

parka (PARK-uh)—a long coat with a hood, traditionally made of caribou or seal skin and lined with fur

residential (rez-i-DEN-shuhl)—relating to where people live

resilience (ri-ZIL-yunhs)—the ability to recover from or adjust to misfortune or change

Read More

Brown, Tricia. *Children of the First People: Fresh Voices of Alaska's Native Kids*. Berkeley, CA: West Margin Press, 2019.

Phillips, Katrina M. *The Disastrous Wrangel Island Expedition*. North Mankato, MN: Capstone, 2022.

Treuer, Anton. *Everything You Wanted to Know About Indians But Were Afraid to Ask*. Hoboken, NJ: Levine Querido, 2021.

Internet Sites

Explore Our Culture
icor.inuuqatigiit.ca/explore-our-culture

ICC Kids
inuitcircumpolar.com/icc-kids

Native People of the Arctic and Subarctic
kids.nationalgeographic.com/history/article/native
-people-of-the-arctic-and-subarctic

Index

About the Author

Tia Puya Tidwell belongs to the Nunamiut people of Anaktuvuk Pass and is a Naqsragmiut tribal member. She is a professor of Alaska Native Studies whose research investigates cultural artifacts produced by settler society in order to understand conceptions of land and belonging and the relationship between imagination and policy. She loves to share Inuit culture, sew atikłuks and parkas for her family, and spend time on the nuna with her dogs.